TO THE WATER'S EDGE

Sam Ragan

Moore Publishing Company
Durham, North Carolina

8/1.5
R/2π
76727
Nov. 1971

For Marjorie

On eve of April mornings . . .

And times of always now.

TO THE WATER'S EDGE

These are the markings that I make.

MARKINGS

These are the markings that I make —
The trees now gold that will be green again,
The stone which brings the horse to halt when
  plowing furrows which must be begun again,
The slope of land to where the willows grow
Along a stream that flows to woods
Where birds now fly.
I make the markings with my eye.
For I have not traveled this road before,
And the markings I make are to remember it by.

A WALK ON THE BEACH

On the beach
The birds go walking —
Ahead of me in my walking.
With each wave a feeding,
A movement to the water's edge,
And then away,
Always away, always returning,
Even as I return
To the water's edge.
But I reach the point of turning back.
The birds go on.

ENCOUNTER BY NIGHT

We came over the ridge
And the headlights caught
The scurrying of furry things
On the road's edge.
Their eyes came back to us.
They there in the darkness,
We here in the darkness.

THE NIGHT WATCHMAN

I see him go his rounds,
His electric lantern casting shadows
On the places he patrols.
The clock is always with him
As he goes at one, at two, at three, at four,
And finally five.
Gray day comes over the rooftops.
He looks at his watch
And turns down the lights.
The watchman goes home and I know
That I too have been a watchman in the night,
Punching many clocks
Of dubious distinction.

THE SNOW MAN

When we've gone beyond the time of returning,
Measured out the wash of wind
And falling rain,
And the snow man's face has faded
There alone in the yard
With the big oak tree,
Holding still the broomstick banner
That was so bright and brave
In the clean new snow,
But now gone, and only the stark stick remains
In clumsy faceless hands,
Growing smaller until they, too, and all
Are gone . . .

I WALK UPON THE WATER

I walk upon the water,
Touching lightly the white spewing waves.
I can see
Downward the sea's sand,
The water is clear and warm.
The sun makes itself known.
I dance.
I dance upon the water,
Seeing seaweed float by.
A fish goes far out to sea.
I am anchored here above the waves.
The sun and me —
We walk upon the water.

THE GIRL IN THE GREEN BATHING SUIT

The girl in the green bathing suit
Swings in a swing near the sea.
I watch from my window.
There's a tree bent by the winds
That hangs over the roof of the house.
I can see through the tree's limbs,
Beyond the girl
In the green bathing suit,
Beyond the sea oats and sand,
Where the sea rolls,
Breaking white, as far out
As where the fishing boat
Sits motionless in the sun.

ESSENTIALS OF A POEM

They must take off from somewhere:
A place, a tree, a stream, a sea.
A point of land, a point of view,
A point of departure, a place
From which the words must go.
Maybe they never get to a stopping place
But go on and on —
It's the journey that counts —
Not getting there,
Bringing words and all to end.
It's starting from somewhere
And going, going, going . . .

DISCOVERY ON THE BEACH

If in turn of tide we should find
Imprint of leaf and bone of man
Long gone from these shores of sun and sea,
Could we tell
How it happened and why
In that day when he, too, ran
Wildly in the sand,
Clutching this leaf as he fell.
Was he also alone?
And did the sea wash out his prints
As they have mine,
And he, looking back, saw no sign
Where he had walked,
Where he had been?

SOUND AND A SEA SHELL

I have been sitting here watching the rain
Fall outside my window.
I hold a shell from the sea.
They say if you put it to your ear
You can hear the sea, the sounds.
But all I hear is rain
This November afternoon.
The inside of the shell is pink.

I SIT ON A PORCH AT NAGS HEAD
IN LATE AFTERNOON AND WATCH THE SEA

Across the sand's ridge
The sea is flat and muffled
In daylight's downward plunge.
There is no wind.
There is no movement in the grass,
No movement in the sea.
I ebb with the tide,
With the sun.
I watch a bird
Dive swiftly
To the water.

LUCKY STARS

Some people, they say, were born under lucky stars.
And I have been searching for my star,
A star that I can walk under
On a summer night,
And point to, saying:
That is my star,
I was born under that star.
And when I do, the star
Will wink back, and say:
"Sure, have it your own way."

LONG DAY'S JOURNEY INTO NIGHT

I have walked long in this night of frozen stars.
My feet make loud sounds,
But no one hears.
They have closed the doors
And drawn the shades.
Even the dog's bark
Is only a whimper.

BIRTHDAY GREETING

You come at time of lilac
And the bloom of plums,
On eve of April mornings
When the world is new
In willow green and birdcall
So near you can reach out
And hold it —
Hold it in your hand
Yours the taking without asking,
Knowing that to give
Is to keep —
To keep forever in other calendar turns
And times of always now.

ANNIVERSARY NOTED

In this time of turnings,
The first yellow leaf
And whisper of haze
Hovering at evening over far trees,
Yet with mid-mornings still
Bright with butterflies —
Yes, at this time of turnings
In the cycles and circles of our seasons
I also turn again
And see with love
The soaring of birds
Over the surf of sea,
And you awakening to sound and touch
That tell me more
Than these and need no words.

HOW LIKE THE ROSE

Walking out this morning,
With the night's rain still
Captured and cupped
In the leaves of trees,
How like the rose
I come upon the dawn.

ON THE WAY TO THE FOOTBALL GAME

On the way to the football game
There was a long line of cars.
The car from Wisconsin
Stopped to let us in.
The movement had come to a halt
And we sat watching
The flood of Fall around us.
There were flowers in the field.
The boys in the car from Wisconsin behind us
Were singing "We don't give a damn for Duke
    University . . ."
Someone sounded an impatient horn.
"Why don't you write something," you said,
    "about the damn yellow daisies."

. . . in the eyes of owls

The darkness is kind.

THOUGHTS ON HEARING
AN OWL'S CRY IN EARLY MORNING

The call came from deep in the woods,
I could only guess its distance,
And what he saw I could not see.
But in the eyes of owls
The darkness is kind.
His Who is answered
But my What, Where, When — and Why.
What are the dreams of owls
Before their blind flight into daylight?

Do all dreams die by day?

VIEW FROM THE BRIDGE
OVER THE CAPE FEAR AT WILMINGTON

On a piling in the river
A sea gull sat.
The river flowed around him.
The sun caught the tide's surge,
And the bird sat hunched in time,
Unmoving as the water moved,
As the sunlight moved.
And I —
Watching the gull, the sun, and the water —
Stood silent and unmoving.

14

THE MARKED AND UNMARKED

I cannot say upon which luminous evening
I shall go out beyond the stars,
To windless spaces and unmarked time,
Turning nights to days and days to nights.

This is the place where I live.
I planted this tree.
I watched it grow.
The leaves fall and I scuff them with my feet.
This is the street on which I walk.
I have walked it many times.
Sometimes it seems there are echoes of my
walking —

In the mornings, in the nights,
In those long evenings of silence and stars

— the unmarked stars.

NIGHT DRIVE IN SNOW

The snow, rutted
By a lone car's passage,
Covers everything,
Making it strange and unfamiliar —
I have long since passed
The place I should have turned.
The snow continues to fall.
I drive on.

OCTOBER STATEMENT

Written in a clear hand
In black ink and xeroxed,
It said:
Purchase of $19.57.
That was all the store sent me
Of its "October Statement."
But I have my own
October Statement to make —
And I find it difficult to contain
In such conciseness and clarity.
For October is a haze,
A blue sky and a cry
Of unnamed things that wing
Beyond the hill that flares
And taunts the eye,
Of stumbling feet, running
To catch something,
Something that was there, but lost,
Lost a long time ago.
But I keep on running —
Running into October.

CRICKETS

The crickets call came from the chimney.
They bring good luck, said the young one.
They eat clothes, said the old one.
And in the silence of the room
An answering call was heard
In the far corner.

16

THE WRITER OF SONGS

He writes strange words
And sings them to himself,
All alone there by the window.
The words are like candy
To be tasted, to be tested on the tongue
Before the placing on the paper.
They are his songs, his poems.
He will carry them in his notebook
And if anyone will listen
He will sing to them
Just as he sings now
To himself.

THE MAN IN THE 7-11 STORE

He does not want me to go.
He sells me things,
And then he talks
Long after the figures
Have been rung up on the cash register.
He wants me to stay,
For when I am gone
He is alone —
Alone in the lights
And the shelves
Of canned goods.
I get lonesome, he says.
I like people
To be around.

MISS MARIANNE MOORE

"I don't call myself a poet," said Marianne Moore.
   "I'm just like anybody else."

Just like anybody else,
With hands that can grasp,
Eyes that can dilate,
Hair that can rise.
That's what poetry is all about, she said.
But the white-haired lady who liked
To cheer the Brooklyn Dodgers
And dream up new names
For Ford automobiles
Also talked about a poet's presenting
Imaginary gardens
With real toads in them —

   Just like anybody else.

NIGHT SOUNDS

   I have climbed the stairs in the darkness
   And listened to the rain
   On the roof and in the trees.
   I sit here listening to other far-off sounds —
   A train is moving southward.
   The cat cries at the doorway.
   I will not let her in.

FACES

They say that Rembrandt
Was fifty years old
When he decided
To devote all his time,
His art,
His strength,
To faces.

We see them now —
Fragile, lumpy, shadowy things,
Each a mystery,
Each a face of its own.
A visible thing, an invisible thing.
We keep coming back
To Rembrandt's faces.

". . . to live is to fight with trolls."—Ibsen.

THAT SUMMER

That summer when the creeks all dried up
Except for a few deep holes
Under the caved-out roots of oaks
Now leaning toward the water's edge.
The catfish clung to the mud
But now and then a perch was caught
In the oatsack seine.
Even the Tar was a trickle
And I could walk all the way across
On the rocks, and the place
Where we had swung from limb to water —
Splashing below surface and rising sputtering
Was now no more than moist mud
From which a turtle crawled.

They sat on the porches
And talked of the weather,
And Herbert Hoover,
Cursing both, and every son of a bitch
Who had voted for him.
Even if the Baptists saved any souls
Worth the saving
Where in the hell would they find the water
To baptize them.

A wild turkey flew out of the woods
And even if it was out of season
He fed a family for two days.
And it was better than that mud turtle
That looked like mud and tasted like mud . . .
that summer when it didn't rain.

A LONG DAY DYING

She picked at embroidered things
On the covers, fingers apart
From eyes that looked out
On an ancient tree, half-fallen
From the wind, at leaves that rippled now and then
In the August afternoon.
"I can tell you," she said . . .
"I can tell you . . ." but then
Her mind went on to other things
Such as how she wanted her supper,
And didn't the geranium Dolly had brought her
Look pretty in the window.
Far down the field the shadows fell
And a dove called from the woods.
Beyond the hill where the road turned
Dust swirled in a slanting sun.
It had been a long day,
A long day dying . . .
"I can tell you," she said,
Her fingers toying with a tuft of flowers.

THE FORGOTTEN

The calendar turns
And days are measured and marked off,
Weeks, months and years,
Then new pages to be torn and thrown away.
The wind carries them away.

The moon has moved from where it began,
The stars are not so bright,
But in the yard a whip-poor-will cries.
The night has long been with us.

She had written:
I never saw another butterfly.
That was all.
An epitaph for the nameless,
The forgotten who cannot be forgotten.

That was the summer of much rain
And the crops could not stand
When the wind came.
By lantern light they worked in the fields,
But it was no use.

The streams were overflowing their banks
A boy was drowned when he went too near.
They saw him holding a willow branch.
It bent with him and he was gone,
The water swirling around the willow.
The last thing seen was his hand.

THE DEATH OF A POET

He had gone out
On that night of rising moon
And early stars,
Walking by the side of the road,
Careful of passing cars,
Their lights on turning leaves,
In the woods where darkness grows.
He kept on walking —
Walking, walking, walking —
And the darkness grew darker.
Down the last road,
Down to the end of the road,
And the last passing car.

MR. IBSEN AND HIS TROLLS

It was natural, I suppose,
For old Henrik Ibsen
To think in terms of trolls.
And he wrote: "to live
    is to fight with trolls . . ."
I have been thinking about that
For a long time —
I have never seen a troll.
But I know what Mr. Ibsen was talking about.

ONE LATE AFTERNOON WHEN TIME ENDED

In the room with the big clock
She talked, and for awhile I listened.
I watched the clock.
Is time a measured thing
Of ticks and tocks and moving hands,
Or shadows from the sun,
Pages torn from the calendar on the wall,
The rings in a tree cut down?

She talked on. The room had grown dark.
The clock had no hands,
There were no numbers on the calendar,
And the sun had gone past shadows.

THE DAY THE HAWK CAME

On that day in summer
When the hawk came,
The hen's cries signaling his coming
Into the chicken yard,
My mother came running
Flapping an apron.
But the hawk had gone,
Carrying the young chicken
Up and over the distant trees.
The sky was a bright blue.
My mother was crying,
And the hens had gone to hide.

BUTTERFLIES

She had run after it
Down the steep lawn
Toward the river, her eyes
Upon the flying thing
Bright upon the sun,
And then the sharp pain,
The sting, and she ran back
Crying.
Her fingers moved as she talked,
She was trying to explain things.
I thought it was a butterfly,
She said, but I could never
Tell butterflies from bees.

THE POET

The poet stood in front of the class
And talked about his poems.
My poems are fragments, he said.
All my life I have gathered fragments.
I try to put them together.
He talked on and on, telling
Pleasant stories — about what
Red Warren said about writing a poem:
Erecting a public monument
From a private itch — and of others
Who also talked about their sullen art.

His talk was in fragments,
And then,
And then the girl in the front row
Uncrossed her legs
And his mind wandered to other things.

FROM HERE TO THERE

Starting out from nowhere,
All the way across the country,
To nothing, nothing, nothing at all.

The years add up,
Hair gone and teeth fallen away,
There's not even a laugh any more . . .

He cries in the long night,
And all night long the cries
And the coo of pigeons
Walking on the tin roof of the porch
Outside his window,
Their feet like small rain,
Even the flutter of their wings
Like rain.
But there was no rain that August,
No rain at all.

27

IN A FIELD HOSPITAL ON OKINAWA

No, no, no, no, no, no —
It did not happen that way.
I was sitting there,
I heard him cry out,
I thought the shell had got me too,
And there were more of them,
Falling, falling, falling . . .
The ten yards were ten miles.
I wanted to go there —
Did I go?
Did I go there,
Did I go there
When he cried out?

A PROFESSOR EXPLAINS A PURCHASE

The professor was sixty-five.
His wife had died, and he sold his sedan
And bought a convertible.
I like to go riding with the top down, he said.
At five o'clock in the morning.
There is no sound,
No sound at all,
And I feel very close
To the late stars and
The sky.

BOXES

The man sits at the window and draws squares.
Inside the larger squares he draws smaller squares.
Looking into them
There is an illusion
Of looking deep into something
That goes on and on
Into something beyond time,
Beyond the mind's eye.
But the man who draws squares
Knows there is nothing there.
They are only lines he has linked together
Into boxes — boxes within boxes —
Boxes without tops,
Boxes without bottoms.

. . . star-fixed

In meadows of larksong and dancing daisies.

FROTHY HAZARDS

Many years before Neil Armstrong
Stepped upon the moon
There had been speculation by the scientists,
And one headline read:
"Moon Pictures Hint Frothy Hazards."
But this had been said long ago,
Before even the cries on Crete
In the dark meadows of time's fitful starts —
They knew the hazards of madness
Stalking the unwary wanderers
In the falling mists of moonlight.
They said that they who were flecked
By the moon's froth
Were the happy doomed ones,
Wandering earth-bound
But star-fixed
In meadows of larksong and dancing daisies.

SUMMER SOUTH

Even now in September
The crepe myrtle blooms.
This land forever seeks
Summer. It holds it tightly
In its hand, and with hoarse voice
Proclaims it as its own.
The reds dominate,
Bright reds in waning green.

31

THEY DRIVE BY NIGHT

Bring it on down to my house, honey —

Yeah.
He wipes the counter and stares.
The lights go by
On the highway.

Ain't nobody home but me.

Two o'clock —
The son of a bitch must be doing ninety.
And there's a god-damned fly
In the pie case.

Ain't nobody home but me.

THE HEBREWS

In Hebrew, I am told, there is no present tense.
It's always past,
Sometimes future,
Never now.

And what does that tell us about the Hebrews?

THE END OF SUMMER

All the way
From Currituck to Calabash
There's yet one last turn to the sea.
They fish all night
From the piers at Wrightsville,
Casting again and again
Where moon flecks waves.
They are those who have fled the world,
One hundred yards into the sea.
And there are those who cannot turn loose from
    summer.
They walk alone,
Searching the horizon off Hatteras,
One last climb up Jockey Ridge,
Toward a red-fingered sky
Beyond the shadowed slopes.

In this late slanting sun
The pipers run ahead
Of the walker to the water's edge,
They eat and run
From the curl of the sea.
They go on
But the walker turns to other sounds
And the sweep of wind across the sand.

The others have all gone
With the end of summer.
Summer's end comes
On fog wisps and bird's cry.

A MOMENT IN TIME
WHEN THE WHOLE WORLD WAS BLUE

A lone butterfly
Came to the crevice
Where a flower grew.
Poised there on the side of the mountain,
Blue wings between
Blue flowers,
Blue sky.

THE SLANT OF THE SNOW

It's the wind's drive
Pushing past the trees
That gives us the slant
Of the snow
Falling.

WINTER WATCH

In those winter fields
Where only the dead grass
Hides the movement of mice
And the loping fox long away
From hunters, horn and dog,
Walking and watching wind bend
Bare branches at the wood's edge.
This then is the beginning,
The walk and the waiting,
Winter is a time of waiting,
The pause, the slowed feet,
The watching, the waiting.

SPRING INVENTORY

There are some leaves left
From the fall's raking,
And many clogged drains
Needing a quick April rain
To wash them clean.
The first tentative green
Comes from the willow,
But the lilac is bare of buds
And the wind's sting
Still speaks of sterile spring.

IN THE DARK PLACES

You can find them in the dark places.
Under the leaves,
Where the moss is damp.
You come upon them suddenly,
And their blue is a violent thing.
One never thinks of violets
Being so violent.

ONE MOMENT ON AN AUGUST AFTERNOON

The green vine hangs on the hidden wall.
A forgotten flower has come forth
To receive the hummingbird's pause.
The sun's gone past
The hickory tree.
The shadows fall across the yard.
A white cat yawns,
And a bird
Resumes its singing.

I don't know Charlie,

And Charlie doesn't know me.

NOTES ON THE MARGINS OF OUR TIMES

Driving down No. 1 at night
The headlights catch the gleam
Of beer cans.
They look like cat's eyes.

When lilacs last by the junkyard bloomed.

The clenched fist, the angry eye.
Does the shout hide hurt?
And from the west the smoke
Of a city burning.

When Johnny comes marching . . .

At the edge of the crowd
The old man watches and
Hears the distant voices
Cry out against war.

O say can you see . . .

And in the Mekong Delta
The captain speaks matter-of-factly:
We had to destroy it
To save it.

What so proudly we hailed . . .

In the Yadkin the white bellies
Of fish float
Upon the water.
They shine in the moonlight.
In Los Angeles they cry
And vomit upon the streets.

Raindrops keep falling on my head.

The soldier squats in the jungle dark,
Holding his rifle in his hand.
Charlie's out there —
I don't know Charlie,
And Charlie doesn't know me,
But we're going to kill each other.

First in war, first in peace . . .

The crowd gathers where the flags fly
Around the tall monument.
They shout obscenities
At the people below.
A folk singer sings
How long, O Lord, how long.

Give us your tired, your huddled poor.

The river caught fire,
Too wet to plow, too thick to drink.
And the rats chewed away
The baby's face.

The Age of Aquarius.

Hair covered their faces,
Hung down their backs.
And the men in tin hats
Left them matted in blood.

Do not go bojangles into that good night.

You may talk of ginger beer
When you're quartered safe out here . . .
And he talked so loud
I couldn't hear a word he said.

This is my country . . .

On I-95 the cars go by —
70, 80, 90 miles an hour.
The fields are filled with weeds,
And kudzu covers the house.
A man and a mule are silhouettes of the sun.
He's the last one left.
In Wilson the man says:
I fed barbecue to fifteen thousand.

A summer land where the sun doth shine.

They ran laughing into the water,
The sea curled white against their knees.
And under the tall pines

The red fox ran
Without the sound
Of hunter's horn.

This Guy's in Love With You

The brass is a fine sure sound.
In Tiajuana they sell all sorts of things
On the street corners.
And on the way back
They stop your car
For you to declare your purchase.

Shine On, Shine On, Harvest Moon

Everybody watched the walk,
The gathering of rocks.
And at Cape Kennedy
They built the launcher
Away from the nest
Of the last bald eagle.

Come, Josephine, in My Flying Machine

It was a bad trip,
And when he couldn't fly
They picked up his body
Where it had splintered on the sidewalk.

Heaven's Blessings Attend Her

He lookéd out upon a sea of faces.
They were asking questions.
He could hear them
But he did not have any answers.

O give me a home . . .

Paul Green tells of the dream
In "The Lost Colony" and under the stars
Each summer on Roanoke Island
The dream is re-lived
For all the lost and lonely.
And in the dark woods
The phantom eyes cry out
Against the invaders,
The spoilers.

Look Away, Look Away, Dixie Land

The little man rides a bicycle
Backwards. He gives away
Ax handles as souvenirs.
And the flamingoes fly
Into the sunset.

I Want to Hold Your Hand

The blind man sits and plays the guitar.
Sometimes a dime is dropped into his cup.
The fat man with the cigar
Rides in a car that says:
"America — Love it or Leave it."

Music I heard with you . . .

A whip-poor-will calls from the valley.
It is a night of stars,
And the wind's sound in the pines
Is the sound of the sea.